The NEW MEXICO Journey

# STUDENT GUIDE

GIBBS SMITH EDUCATION
TO ENRICH AND INSPIRE HUMANKIND

19  18  17  16  15  14  13  12          1  2  3  4  5

Published by
Gibbs Smith Education
P.O. Box 667
Layton, UT 84041
800.748.5439
education.gibbs-smith.com

Supervising Curriculum Developer: Megan Hansen Moench
Curriculum Developers: Kristi Toponce, Carolee Calvin
Editorial Assistants: Juliana Garrett, Hollie Keith, Charlene Kerwin Reyes
Cover Design: John Vehar
Production Designer: Alan Connell

Because these websites are maintained by other organizations, Gibbs Smith Education is not responsible
for their content. When book was printed, however, all of the website addresses
were functioning and the content was appropriate for students.

Gibbs Smith books are printed on either recycled, 100% post-consumer waste, FSC-certified papers,
or on paper produced from a 100% certified sustainable forest/controlled wood source.

Printed and bound in the United States of America
ISBN13: 978-1-4236-1607-8

# STUDENT GUIDE

## CONTENTS

**What Is History?** Lesson **1**                                        **Activator**

## Putting the Picture Together

Your teacher will hand you one or two pieces of a puzzle. Look only at your pieces and write down what you think the whole picture will be.

Your guess: _____

_____

Get together with the other members of your group. Share your guess with the other members of your group. Now complete the puzzle and answer the following questions.

1. Was the picture what you predicted? _____

2. Did anyone in your group correctly guess what the picture was with only their pieces?

   _____

3. Did people's guesses show their biases (did the guesses have to do with anything that they

   liked or were interested in)? If so, how?

   _____

   _____

4. Did you need to have every piece in place to know what the picture was? Why or why not?

   _____

 **What Is History?**   Lesson  **1**   **Key Terms**

Fill in the Key Term that matches the definition. Then use the circled letters to complete the phrase that tells the category the Key Terms fall into.

1. A one-sided point of view

   __ (__) __ __

   | |
   | --- |
   | artifact |
   | bias |
   | oral history |
   | perspective |
   | primary source |
   | secondary source |

2. An understanding of events and people based on the accepted ideas and values of the time period being studied

   __ __(__)__ __ __ __ __ __ __ __

3. An objects made by people or used in the past

   __ __(__)__ __ __ __ __ __

4. An account or summary of an event based on the study of one or more primary sources; a secondhand account of an event

   __ __ __ __ __ __ __ __ (__)__ __ __ __ __

5. A firsthand, or eyewitness, account or original object or document from the past

   __ __ __ __ __ __ __  __(__)__ __ __ __

6. Spoken history that one person tells to another

   __ __ __ __ (__)__ __ __ __ __(__)

**Use the circled letters to form the answer to this question:**

7. All the Key Terms from this lesson are tools of __ __ __ __ __ __ __ .

**What Is History?**          Lesson **1**          **Comprehension Strategy**

## Preview Images

Complete this chart as you preview the images in the lesson. Revisit this chart after reading to see if your guesses were correct.

| Page # | Description of Image | What it tells you about the lesson | Check if your guess was right |
|---|---|---|---|
|  |  |  |  |
|  |  |  |  |
|  |  |  |  |
|  |  |  |  |
|  |  |  |  |
|  |  |  |  |

**Application**

## Write from Another Point of View

Complete the organizer to help you tell about an event from your partner's point of view.

| | |
|---|---|
| **Who was there?** | _____<br>_____<br>_____ |
| **What happened?** | _____<br>_____<br>_____ |
| **Were you a part of this event?** | _____<br>_____<br>_____ |
| **What role did you play?** | _____<br>_____<br>_____ |
| **Why did it happen?** | _____<br>_____<br>_____ |
| **How did you feel?** | _____<br>_____<br>_____ |

**The Geographer's View**    Lesson     **Activator**

## Where Are You?

Sketch a simple map to show where you are located in each of the following places.

| | |
|---|---|
| Classroom | School |
| City | State |
| Continent | Planet |

**The Geographer's View**    Lesson  2                    **Key Terms**

Draw a line to match each Key Term to the correct definition.

**1.** The exact position of a place using longitude and latitude coordinates

**2.** A reference line that runs through Greenwich, England, and divides the world into eastern and western hemispheres

**3.** The description of where a place is in relation to other places or things

**4.** The measurement of distances north and south of the equator

**5.** The study of the earth's land, water, people, plants, and animals, and how they relate to one another

**6.** Half of the earth

**7.** The measurement of distances east and west of the prime meridian

**8.** Places on earth that have at least one common physical, human, or cultural feature

**A.** absolute location

**B.** geography

**C.** hemisphere

**D.** latitude

**E.** regions

**F.** longitude

**G.** prime meridian

**H.** relative location

The Geographer's View    Lesson **2**    **Comprehension Strategy**

## Preview Key Ideas

Help create a skit to describe the Key Idea your teacher will assign you. Use this organizer to take notes of the skits for the other Key Ideas.

| Key Idea | Sections from Student Edition related to skit | How the skit represented the Key Idea |
|---|---|---|
| | | |
| | | |
| | | |
| | | |

**The Geographer's View**   Lesson  **2**                    **Application** (page 1 of 2)

## Opinions on Your Location

Respond to the following questions or prompts.

1. Name two ways to pinpoint the exact location of your home on the earth.

   _____

   _____

2. List five things you like about the place where you live (not just your home, but your neighborhood or town, too).

   _____

   _____

   _____

   _____

   _____

3. List five things you would change about the place where you live.

   _____

   _____

   _____

   _____

   _____

4. List three ways you have helped protect your environment.

   _____

   _____

   _____

The Geographer's View    Lesson     **Application** (page 2 of 2)

**5.** List three ways you have harmed your environment.

_____

_____

_____

**6.** Can you change any of the harmful ways you have interacted with the environment to be helpful or neutral?

_____

_____

**7.** What do you like about living in the Southwest region?

_____

_____

**8.** What would you change about life in the Southwest region?

_____

_____

**9.** Would you ever consider moving out of the Southwest region? Why or why not?

_____

_____

## Do You Know New Mexico?

Working together in pairs, see how many provinces, mountains, rivers, and cities of New Mexico you already know. Which ones do you still need to learn about? Create a legend as you complete your map.

**Provinces**
Rocky Mountains
Colorado Plateau
Great Plains
Basin and Range

**Mountains**
San Juan
Sangre De Cristo
Zuni
San Francisco
Black
San Andres
Sacramento

**Rivers**
Rio Grande
Gila
Pecos
Canadian
San Juan

**Cities**
Sante Fe
Las Cruces
Albuquerque
Carlsbad
Farmington
Your Town

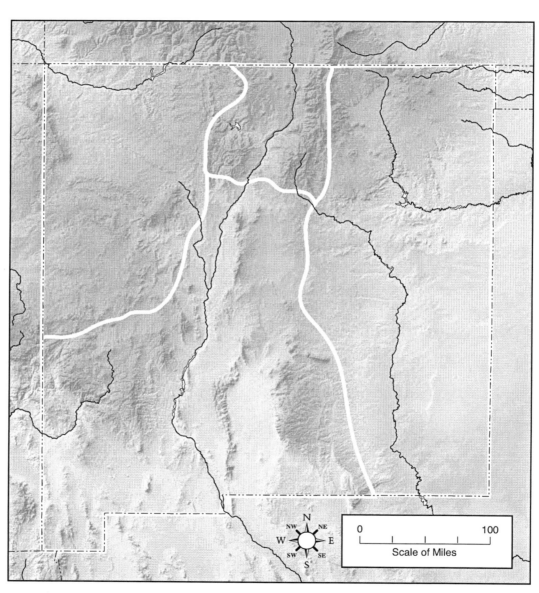

**LEGEND**

**A Tour of New Mexico**   Lesson    **Key Terms**

## Key Terms Crossword

Answer the clues to fill in the crossword puzzle.

| | |
|---|---|
| butte | plateau |
| demography | province |
| Llano Estacado | reservoir |
| malpais | tributary |
| mesa | |

### Across

**2.** an area of land with unique features as well as distinct plants and animals

**3.** a hill that has steep sloping sides and a flat top; similar to a mesa but smaller

**5.** the study of the characteristics of human populations, such as size, growth, and density (number of people per square mile)

**7.** an elevated area of mostly flat land usually extending from a mountain range; a tableland

**8.** a stream or smaller river that flows into a larger body of water, such as a river or lake

**9.** meaning "table" in Spanish; refers to an elevated land form that is so flat on top that it looks like a tabletop

### Down

**1.** meaning "staked plains" in Spanish; refers to a dry, treeless area covering more than 30,000 square miles in eastern New Mexico and western Texas

**4.** a natural or manmade pond or lake used for storing water

**6.** a landform characterized by its fields of dried lava

## Preview Key Terms

Complete a section of the organizer for eight Key Terms. Use a dictionary or the **Student Edition** glossary if you need help.

| Key Term _____ | Key Term _____ |
|---|---|
| Related Words _____ _____ | Related Words _____ _____ |
| Possible Topics _____ _____ | Possible Topics _____ _____ |
| Actual Topics _____ _____ | Actual Topics _____ _____ |
| Key Term _____ | Key Term _____ |
| Related Words _____ _____ | Related Words _____ _____ |
| Possible Topics _____ _____ | Possible Topics _____ _____ |
| Actual Topics _____ _____ | Actual Topics _____ _____ |

A Tour of New Mexico          Lesson           **Comprehension Strategy** (page 2 of 2)

Key Term
_____

Related Words
_____
_____

Possible Topics
_____
_____

Actual Topics
_____
_____

Key Term
_____

Related Words
_____
_____

Possible Topics
_____
_____

Actual Topics
_____
_____

Key Term
_____

Related Words
_____
_____

Possible Topics
_____
_____

Actual Topics
_____
_____

Key Term
_____

Related Words
_____
_____

Possible Topics
_____
_____

Actual Topics
_____
_____

## Postcards from around the State

Design a postcard of your favorite province in New Mexico. On the front, draw a picture to represent that province or a place within that province. On the back, tell a friend about the province or place within the province. Include details about where it is located in New Mexico.

**Prehistoric People**  Lesson **1**  **Activator**

## Dig It!

Use the grid to make a plan of where you will dig. As you locate "artifacts," record where you find them on the grid.

| | | | |
|---|---|---|---|
| | | | |
| | | | |
| | | | |
| | | | |

**Prehistoric People** Lesson  **Key Terms**

Use the clues below to unscramble each Key Term.

**1. telrucu**

_____ is the beliefs and customs of a group of people.

**2. namo**

A small stone used with a metate by prehistoric people to grind seeds is a

_____.

**3. amette**

A flat stone used with mano by prehistoric people to grind seeds is a

_____.

**4. lalatt**

An _____ is a wooden tool used by Archaic people to throw spears.

**5. opela**

_____ means ancient.

**6. scepriritoh**

The time period before there were written records is called _____.

**7. donam**

A person who moves from place to place is a _____.

**8. egolayrocha**

The study of past people and cultures through a careful examination of artifacts is called

_____.

**9. ginsinodue**

_____ means native.

**Prehistoric People** Lesson  **Comprehension Strategy**

## Preview to Check Facts

Before reading the lesson, write whether you think the statements about New Mexico are true or false. Look for details about the statements as you read. After reading, revisit this page to mark whether statements are true or false. Correct false statements to make them true.

| Response Before Reading | Statements About Prehistoric People | Response After Reading |
|---|---|---|
| | The first people to live in this region were the Paleo people, who lived long before recorded history. | |
| | The first people relied mostly on farming and ranching for food. | |
| | The discovery at Folsom tells us that the earliest people lived in tall, multi-level houses. | |
| | Archaeologists can learn a lot about the first people in this region by studying the items they left behind. | |
| | The Paleo people stayed in this region and became ancestors of some of the people in the region today. | |
| | Archaic people lived in different places during different seasons to hunt different animals. | |
| | The earliest known farmers were the Archaic people. | |
| | Archaic people lived in teepees and took them with them as they traveled. | |
| | Atlatls were a type of rifle used in hunting large animals. | |
| | Researchers have found many baskets that suggest Archaic people used them for many different purposes. | |

## Archaeology in the Garbage

If archaeologists were to look at the garbage from your house this past month, what kinds of things could they learn about you and your family? Fill in each box with some of the things that your trash tells about you according to each category.

**Food**

**Entertainment**

**Tools**

**Clothing**

**Sicknesses**

**Pueblo Farmers**    Lesson **2**    **Activator**

## Details about My Life

Complete the page with details about your life.

| My name: _____ | How I got my name: _____ _____ |
|---|---|
| Where I live: _____ _____ _____ | What I eat: _____ _____ _____ |

Family traditions: _____
_____
_____
_____
_____
_____
_____

Interesting facts about my family: _____
_____
_____
_____
_____
_____
_____
_____

**Pueblo Farmers**      Lesson                               **Key Terms**

Draw a picture to represent each of the Key Terms. Use three terms in each box. Using the same Key Terms from the picture, write a paragraph using the terms correctly.

| kiva | monotheism | pueblo |
| matriarchal | polytheism | centralized government |

**Pueblo Farmers**     Lesson **2**     **Comprehension Strategy**

## Preview to Make Predictions

Preview the lesson before reading. Use the chart to make predictions about the lesson and record details about your predictions. After reading, revisit this page to check your predictions and discuss them with a partner.

| Page # | What I previewed | Prediction | Was the prediction right? |
|---|---|---|---|
| | | | |

## Mogollon, Ancestral Puebloan, and Us

List the similarities and differences between the Mogollon, Ancestral Puebloan, and our culture today in food, housing, work, and art.

| | Mogollon | Ancestral Puebloan | Us |
|---|---|---|---|
| **FOOD** | Similar:<br><br>Different: | Similar:<br><br>Different: | Similar:<br><br>Different: |
| **HOUSING** | Similar:<br><br>Different: | Similar:<br><br>Different: | Similar:<br><br>Different: |
| **WORK** | Similar:<br><br>Different: | Similar:<br><br>Different: | Similar:<br><br>Different: |
| **ART** | Similar:<br><br>Different: | Similar:<br><br>Different: | Similar:<br><br>Different: |

**Activator**

## Choices Define Who We Are

Read each scenario and think about how each career would affect your future. Explain the ways your life would change if you had each career.

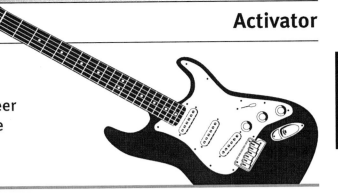

**1.** What might your life be like if you chose to become a musician?

_____

_____

_____

**2.** What might your life be like if you chose to become a nurse?

_____

_____

_____

**3.** What might your life be like if you chose to become a mechanic?

_____

_____

_____

**4.** What might your life be like if you chose to become a lawyer?

_____

_____

_____

**5.** What might your life be like if you chose to become a famous movie star?

_____

_____

_____

**Non-Pueblo Indians**    Lesson     **Key Terms**

Write a definition for each of the Key Terms in your own words. Then use each Key Term in a sentence that shows the meaning of the word.

### 1. Athabascan

Definition: _____

Sentence: _____

_____

### 2. Diné

Definition: _____

Sentence: _____

_____

### 3. hogan

Definition: _____

Sentence: _____

_____

### 4. teepee

Definition: _____

Sentence: _____

_____

### 5. wickiup

Definition: _____

Sentence: _____

_____

Non-Pueblo Indians    Lesson ❸    **Comprehension Strategy**

## Preview to Write Questions

Preview the headings and subheadings in the lesson. Complete the organizer by recording the headings and subheadings and turning them into questions. As you read, look for details to help answer your questions. Revisit this page during and after reading the lesson to record answers to your questions. Mark any questions that were not answered by the lesson.

| Heading/Subheading | Question | Answer |
|---|---|---|
|  |  |  |

Use with *The New Mexico Journey*

## What's the Difference?

Use information from the lesson to complete each section.

List four characteristics that are unique to the Navajo people.

1. _____

2. _____

3. _____

4. _____

List four characteristics that are unique to the Apache people.

1. _____

2. _____

3. _____

4. _____

List four characteristics that are similar between the Navajo and Apache people.

1. _____

2. _____

3. _____

4. _____

## Explorer's Letter

Imagine that you have been invited to take a tour of a new land! Write a letter back home describing your experiences.

Answer the following questions in your letter:

- What did the you see?
- How did the native people react to you being in their land?
- How did you treat the native people?
- Would you live there if you could?
- Did you leave anything in the new land? If so, what?
- Did you bring anything back from that land? If so, what?

**Explorers and Invaders**   Lesson    **Key Terms**

Complete the KIM chart with a **key** idea, additional **information,** and a **memory** clue for each Key Term. The first example is done for you.

|  | **K**ey Idea | Additional **I**nformation | **M**emory Clue |
|---|---|---|---|
| astronomy | study of the universe | stars, moon, planets |  |
| conquistadors |  |  |  |
| epidemic |  |  |  |
| smallpox |  |  |  |
| tribute |  |  |  |

## Text-to-Self Connections

Look for connections between your life and the lives of people in this lesson. Complete the page with information about connections you made while reading.

**1.** How many connections did you make between the text and yourself? _____

**2.** How did making connections change the way you read the lesson?

_____

_____

**3.** Choose the two strongest connections you made in the lesson. Describe each of the connections.

**Connection 1:**

_____

_____

_____

**Connection 2:**

_____

_____

_____

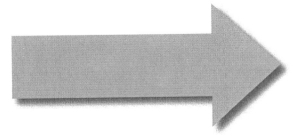
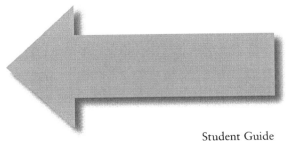

## Conquering Perspectives

From the lesson, choose an empire in the Americas that was conquered by Spain. Use information from the lesson to write a short journal entry from the point of view of three different people who were involved in the conquering of that empire.

**Person #1** _____

_____

_____

_____

**Person #2** _____

_____

_____

_____

**Person #3** _____

_____

_____

_____

## Cities of Gold

Write a short story about what it would be like to live in one of the Seven Cities of Cibola. Be specific and give details.

_____

_____

_____

_____

_____

_____

_____

_____

_____

_____

_____

_____

_____

_____

Complete a word web for each Key Term. Fill the surrounding circles with words that describe or relate to the term.

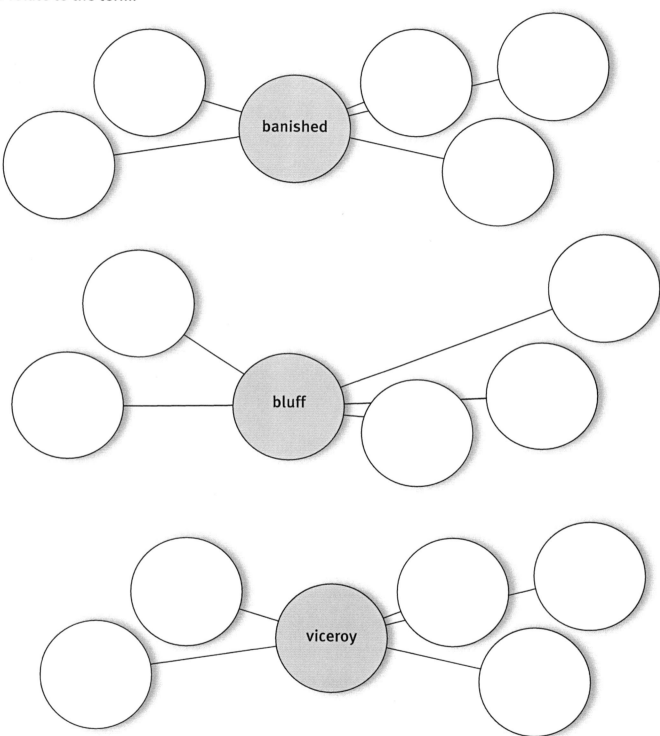

## Text-to-Text Connections

Look for connections between the text and other texts you have read. Complete the page with information about connections you made while reading.

**1.** How many connections did you make between the text and other texts? _____

**2.** How did making connections change the way you read the lesson?

_____

_____

**3.** Choose the two strongest connections you made in the lesson. Describe each of the connections.

**Connection 1:**

_____

_____

_____

_____

**Connection 2:**

_____

_____

_____

_____

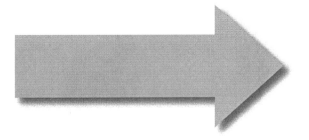 

CHAPTER 3

## Expedition Gossip

Write a gossip column for the local newspaper about the expeditions to New Mexico. Include information and details from the lesson.

### The News

_____          _____

_____          _____

_____          _____

_____          _____

_____          _____

_____          _____

_____          _____

_____          _____

_____          _____

Colonial New Mexico    Lesson  3    **Activator**

CHAPTER 3

## If I Were to Rule

Imagine you run an entire community! Fill in each box explaining how you would rule your own community.

### Laws to keep people safe

### Laws to keep things fair

### Things the community needs

### How I would enforce the laws

**Colonial New Mexico** Lesson  **3**                    Key Terms

Complete the table with information about the Key Terms from this lesson.

| Key Terms | Words to Describe | Examples |
|---|---|---|
| acequia | | |
| cabildo | | |
| mayordomo | | |
| presidio | | |
| refugee | | |
| regidores | | |
| vigas | | |

Colonial New Mexico    Lesson **3**                    # Comprehension Strategy

## Text-to-World Connections

Look for connections between the text and events or issues in the world as you read. Complete the page with information about connections you made while reading.

1. How many connections did you make between the text and the world? _____

2. How did making connections change the way you read the lesson?

_____

_____

3. Choose the two strongest connections you made in the lesson. Describe each of the connections.

**Connection 1:**

_____

_____

_____

_____

**Connection 2:**

_____

_____

_____

_____

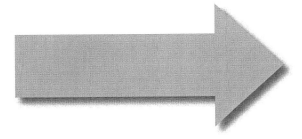

CHAPTER 3

Colonial New Mexico    Lesson  3    **Application**

## Letter From Santa Fe

**Imagine you were there to witness all of the events from this lesson. Write a letter home describing what you saw and what you learned.**

### HEADING

**The date of my letter** _____
Write the date in the top-left section of the letter.

### GREETING

**My letter will be written to** _____
Include a greeting such as *Dear* with the name of the person you are writing to.

### BODY OF LETTER

What did you see?

_____

What did you hear?

_____

What did you feel?

_____

What did you learn?

_____

What event do you think is the most important to this time period?

_____

### CLOSING

Be sure to close your letter with a salutation such as *Sincerely* and sign your name.
Write a final draft of your letter on another sheet of paper.

## Mexico's Fortune Teller

Fill out the graphic organizer by writing Mexico's fortune. Explain what you believe will happen now that Mexico has won its independence from Spain. Answer the questions to help you write your fortune.

*What changes will happen?*

*Who will lead the new republic?*

*Is independence the right thing for Mexico?*

*Will everyone accept the new leadership and new changes?*

The Republic of Mexico    Lesson  1                          **Key Terms** (page 1 of 2)

Draw a picture of a Key Term in the middle of the frame. Write the Key Term in the upper-right section. Write the definition for the Key Term in the upper-left section. List some words that describe the term in the lower-left section. Write any synonyms for the term in the lower-right section.

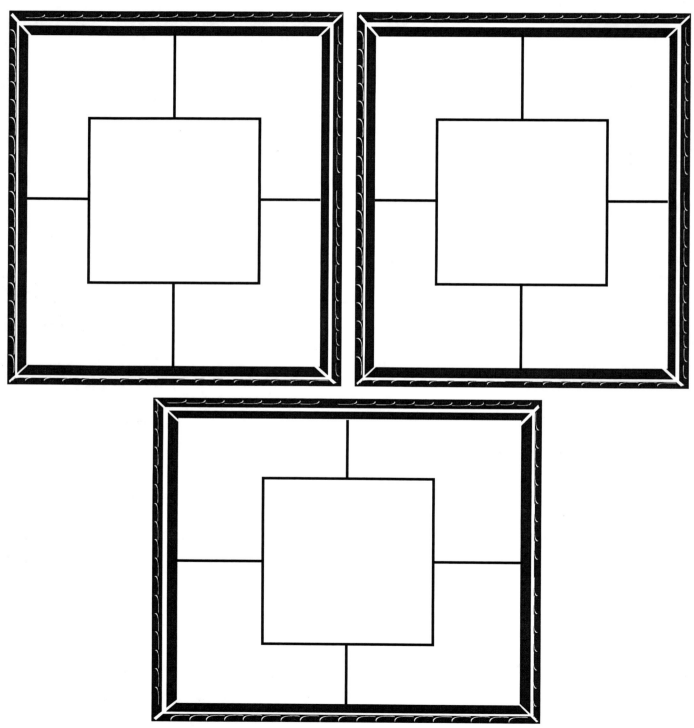

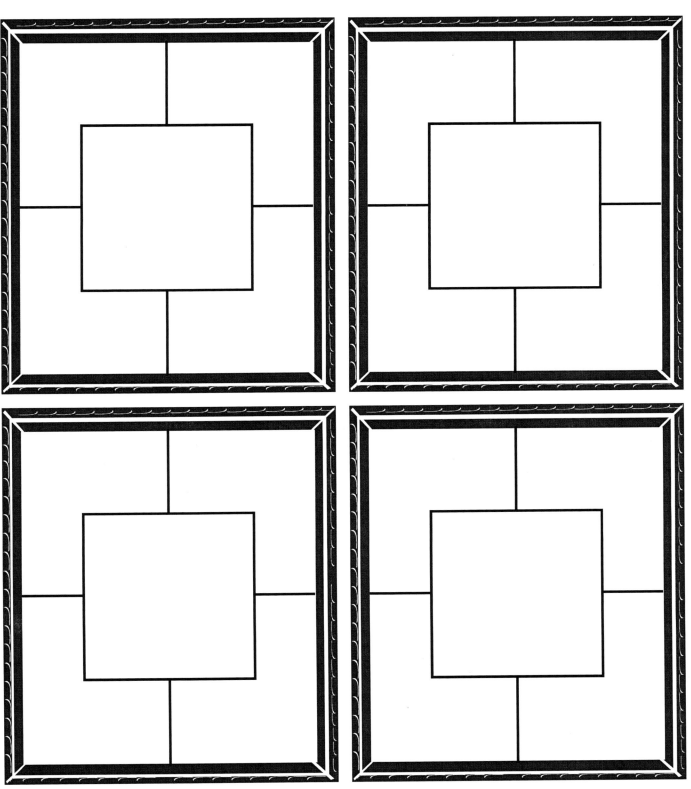

The Republic of Mexico    Lesson  1          Comprehension Strategy

## Question the Text

Use the chart to list questions you have as you read Lesson 2. Write the page and paragraph numbers of where your question came from in the lesson. Then work with a partner to discuss answers to the questions you wrote.

| Page and Paragraph Number | Questions | Answers |
|---|---|---|
| | | |

The Republic of Mexico    Lesson  1    **Application**

CHAPTER 4

## Mexico's Truth Tellers

Using information found in the lesson, explain some of the changes Mexico experienced after they gained independence. Answer the questions to help write your explanation.

What changes happened?

Who was the leader of the new republic?

Was independence the right thing for Mexico?

Did everyone accept the new leadership and new changes?

## Word Splash

Use the words or phrases in the splashes to write a paragraph about what you think this lesson will be about.

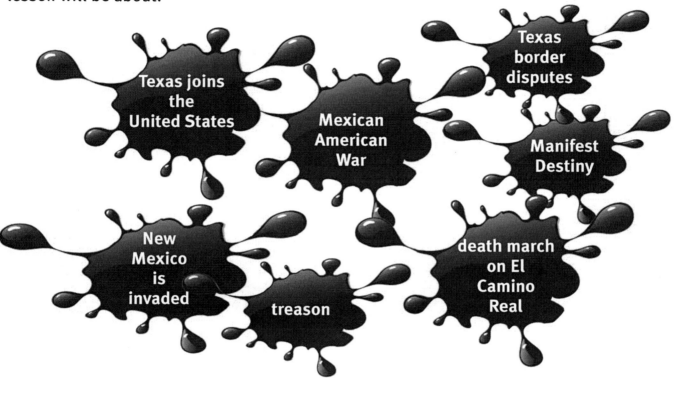

_____

_____

_____

_____

_____

_____

Complete each sentence by connecting each Key Term to something in your life that the word reminds you of. One example is done for you. Use that term again to come up with a different connection!

1. I can connect *annex* to <u>remodeling my house last year</u>

   because <u>we added a larger kitchen and dining room to the house</u>.

2. I can connect *annex* to _____

   because _____.

3. I can connect *cede* to _____

   because _____.

4. I can connect *Manifest Destiny* to _____

   because _____.

5. I can connect *treason* to _____

   because _____.

Choose two Key Terms and explain how they connect to one another.

_____

_____

_____

_____

_____

_____

CHAPTER 4

Mexican American War    Lesson     **Comprehension Strategy**

## Ask Thick and Thin Questions

After reading the lesson, choose two thick and two thin questions you had while reading and write them in the organizer. Write the numbers of the pages that raised the questions. Answer each question, and explain why you think each question is either thick or thin.

| Thick Question | Page Number |
|---|---|
| | |

| Answer to Question | Why Is It Thick? |
|---|---|
| | |

| Thick Question | Page Number |
|---|---|
| | |

| Answer to Question | Why Is It Thick? |
|---|---|
| | |

| Thin Question | Page Number |
|---|---|
| | |

| Answer to Question | Why Is It Thin? |
|---|---|
| | |

| Thin Question | Page Number |
|---|---|
| | |

| Answer to Question | Why Is It Thin? |
|---|---|
| | |

**Mexican American War**   Lesson    **Application**

## War Summary

Fill in the graphic organizer with a summary about the Mexican American War. In the left box, explain how the Mexican American War started, and in the right box, explain how the war ended. Be sure to include causes and effects of the war.

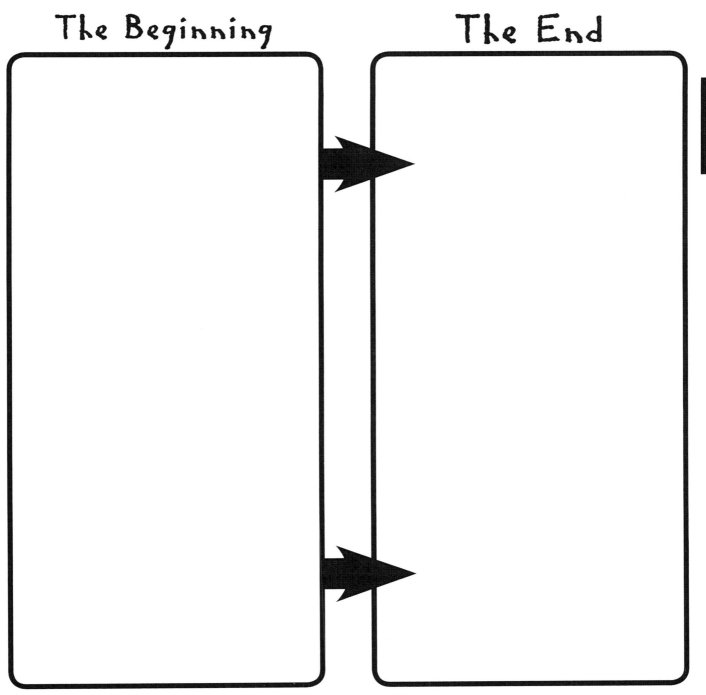

The Beginning

The End

CHAPTER 4

## Worth Fighting For

Make a list of some of your traditions, activities, and beliefs that you would be willing to fight for, and explain why you would be willing to fight for them.

_____

_____

_____

_____

_____

_____

_____

_____

_____

**A Time of War**    Lesson **3**                                    **Key Terms**

Using the Key Terms from the Word Bank, unscramble the terms below. Then write a short story using each of the Key Terms.

1. niarsreevto _____

2. msalteaiis _____

3. cinslsmiaote _____

4. aeslv scdeo _____    _____

> **Word Bank**
>
> assimilate        sectionalism
> reservation       slave codes

CHAPTER 4

_____

_____

_____

_____

_____

_____

_____

_____

_____

_____

_____

_____

A Time of War          Lesson  3          **Comprehension Strategy**

## Sort Your Questions

Fill in the graphic organizer with questions you have from the lesson. Fill in answers to the questions and code each question according to the Code Bank at the bottom of the page.

| Questions | Answers | Code |
|---|---|---|
|  |  |  |
|  |  |  |
|  |  |  |
|  |  |  |
|  |  |  |
|  |  |  |
|  |  |  |
|  |  |  |

### Code Bank

BK—Background Knowledge    D—Discussion          HUH?—Confusion
I—Inferred from text       RS—Requires Research

**A Time of War**     Lesson **3**                  **Application**

## Wars in Review

Write a newspaper article about the wars discussed in this lesson. Include details from the lesson about how each war affected the people involved in them.

# EDITORIAL PAGE

**Growth and Change**    Lesson **1**    **Activator**

## Snapshots of New Mexico

Fill each frame with a drawing of the changes you think New Mexico experienced after it became a U.S. territory.

  **Growth and Change**    Lesson **1**                                    **Key Terms**

Complete the KIM chart with a **key** idea, additional **information,** and a **memory** clue for each Key Term. The first example is done for you.

| | **K**ey Idea | **Additional Information** | **M**emory Clue |
|---|---|---|---|
| boomtown | springs up quickly | often based on mining |  |
| conversos | | | |
| homesteader | | | |
| penitent | | | |
| persecution | | | |
| santo | | | |

**Growth and Change** Lesson  **Comprehension Strategy (page 1 of 2)**

## Take Mental Snapshots

As you read the lesson, stop at certain points and draw a quick sketch of what you visualized. Pay close attention as you read to watch for descriptive words and phrases.

Page_____

Page_____

Page_____

Page_____

CHAPTER 5

Page_____

Page_____

Page_____

Page_____

Growth and Change   Lesson  1

# Application

## Summary of New Mexico's Growth

Write a paragraph about the changes that happened in New Mexico after it became a U.S. territory. Use the tips below to help you write your paragraph.

**Tips for Writing a Good Paragraph**
- Write a sentence stating the main idea of your paragraph.
- Write 3 to 6 sentences to support the main idea. These sentences should include details from the chapter.
- Write a sentence to conclude your paragraph. This sentence should restate your main idea.

**CHAPTER 5**

_____

_____

_____

_____

_____

_____

_____

_____

_____

_____

## Wild, Wild West

The image shown is one representation of the Wild West. Study the image and answer the questions.

1. How does this image represent the Wild West? Be specific.

   _____

   _____

2. How do the people shown in the image represent the Wild West?

   _____

   _____

3. Do you agree with this representation of the Wild West?

   _____

   _____

**Part of the Wild West** Lesson  **Key Terms**

Write a definition for each of the Key Terms in your own words. Use each Key Term in a sentence that shows the meaning of the word. Then write a paragraph about New Mexico using each of the sentences you wrote.

**1.** corrupt

Definition: _____

Sentence: _____

**2.** posse

Definition: _____

Sentence: _____

**3.** squatter

Definition: _____

Sentence: _____

_____

_____

_____

_____

_____

_____

_____

CHAPTER 5

Part of the Wild West          Lesson  2          **Comprehension Strategy**

## Visualize to Retell

As you read the lesson, visualize the events that you are reading about. Stop at the end of each section and record details about what you visualized in that section. You may choose to draw or write the details.

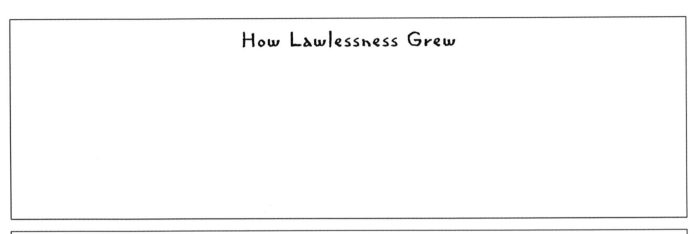

How Lawlessness Grew

Lincoln County War

Land Grants Challenged

**Use what you visualized to write a summary of the lesson on a separate sheet of paper.**

**Part of the Wild West** Lesson **2**

**Application**

## The Wild West!

Create a poster that advertises the Wild West. Create a title and picture for the poster. Write a short summary about the Wild West using information from the lesson.

## We the People

One of the requirements for statehood was to have an approved state constitution that upheld the principles of the U.S. Constitution and guaranteed rights for its citizens. Read the purpose of a constitution as set forth in the Preamble to the U.S. Constitution. Then write the purpose of a constitution in your own words.

> *We the People of the United States, in Order to form a more perfect Union, establish Justice, insure domestic Tranquility, provide for the common defense, promote the general Welfare, and secure the Blessings of Liberty to ourselves and our Posterity, do ordain and establish this Constitution for the United States of America.*

_____

_____

_____

_____

_____

_____

_____

_____

_____

_____

_____

_____

Complete a word web for each Key Term. Fill the surrounding circles with words that describe or relate to the term.

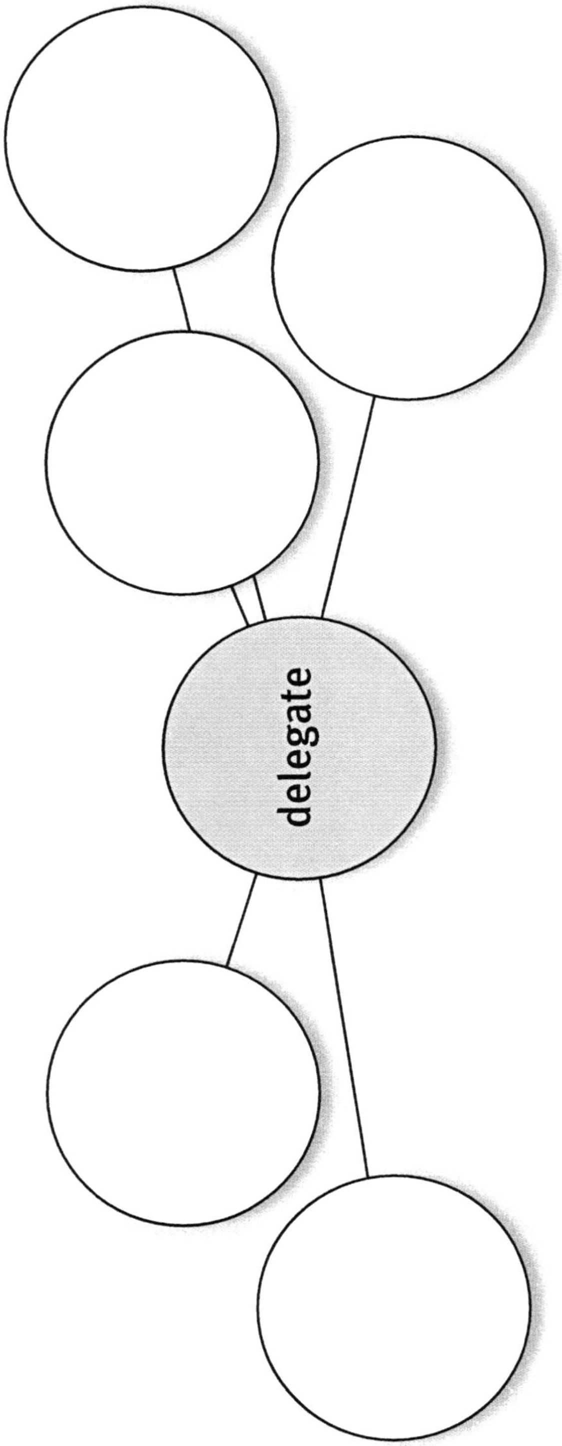

delegate

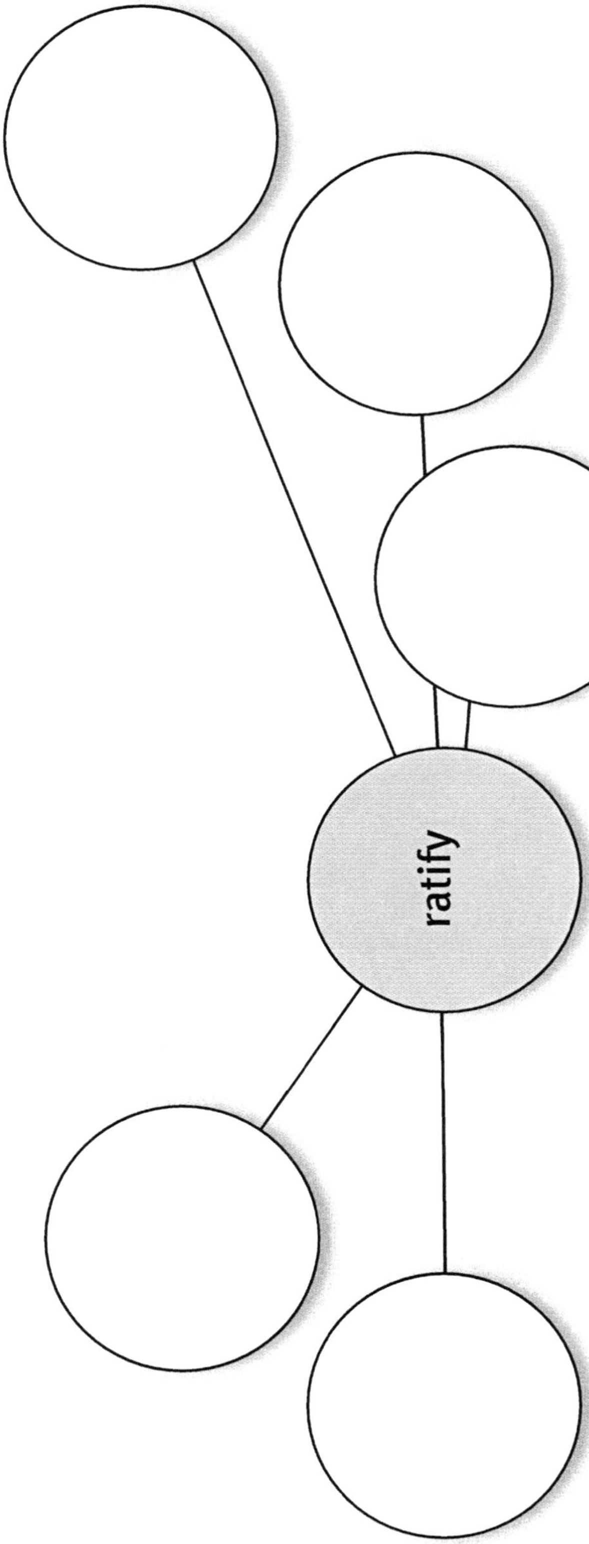

ratify

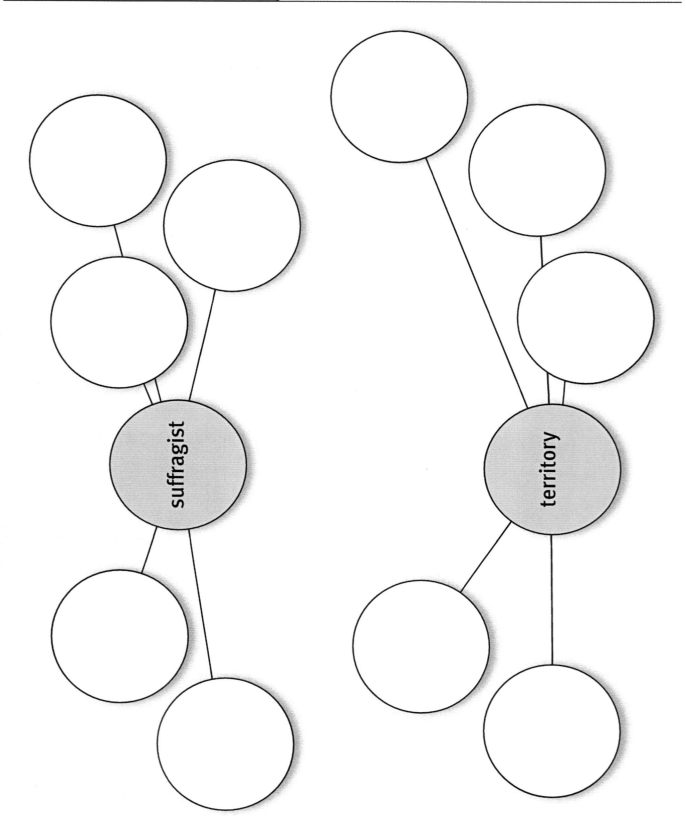

The Struggle for Statehood  Lesson

# Comprehension Strategy

## Use Your Senses

As you read the lesson, imagine the sights, sounds, physical touch, smells, and tastes people from the lesson might have experienced. Record parts of the lesson that appeal to your five senses as you imagine yourself being there.

| | PAGE # |
|---|---|
| **THEY SAW . . .** | |
| **THEY TOUCHED . . .** | |
| **THEY HEARD . . .** | |
| **THEY SMELLED . . .** | |
| **THEY TASTED . . .** | |

CHAPTER 5

## Tanka Poem

Write two tanka poems about two different struggles New Mexico had while becoming a state. Use details and information from the lesson to write your poems.

**TANKA POEM 1** Title: _____

Line 1: Five syllables _____

Line 2: Seven syllables _____

Line 3: Five syllables _____

Line 4: Seven syllables _____

Line 5: Seven syllables _____

**TANKA POEM 2** Title: _____

Line 1: Five syllables _____

Line 2: Seven syllables _____

Line 3: Five syllables _____

Line 4: Seven syllables _____

Line 5: Seven syllables _____

**War, Prosperity, and Depression**   Lesson **1**                                            **Activator**

## Deal or No Deal?

The people in New Mexico had to make some hard choices during World War I and the Great Depression. After playing Deal or No Deal with the class, answer the questions using complete sentences.

1. Was it easy or hard for the class to come to a decision? _____

2. What was the final decision? _____
   _____

3. Did you agree with the final decision? Why or why not? _____
   _____

4. Would you still have made the same choice after seeing what was under all the other cards? Explain. _____
   _____

5. What is the hardest decision you or your family has ever had to make?
   _____
   _____
   _____
   _____
   _____
   _____

CHAPTER 6

**War, Prosperity, and Depression**    Lesson  1    **Key Terms**

Use each Key Term in a sentence about New Mexico's history on the first line. Then use the word in a sentence about your life in New Mexico on the second line.

**1.** depression

a. _____

b. _____

**2.** migrants

a. _____

b. _____

**3.** prosperity

a. _____

b. _____

**4.** public works

a. _____

b. _____

**5.** racism

a. _____

b. _____

**6.** shareholder

a. _____

b. _____

**7.** stock

a. _____

b. _____

# Comprehension Strategy

## Visualize and Infer

As you read, record interesting facts from the lesson. After reading, revisit the facts and combine them with your visualizations to make inference statements about the lesson.

| Facts (something we can see and observe) | What I visualized | Inferences (interpretation) |
|---|---|---|
| | | |

## War, Prosperity, and Depression

Complete each box with information from the lesson. In the first box, explain what is taught in the lesson about war. In the second box, explain what is taught in the lesson about prosperity. In the third box, explain what is taught in the lesson about depression.

> **WAR**

> **PROSPERITY**

> **DEPRESSION**

**New Mexicans Help Win World War II**    Lesson **2**    **Activator**

## Pearl Harbor

President Roosevelt spoke the words below in a radio speech. Work with your group to figure out the meaning of the quote. Start by figuring out the meaning of the word *infamy*. Fill in the information below.

> "December 7, 1941—
> a date which will live in infamy."
>
> —President Roosevelt

Meaning of the prefix "in-":

_____

_____

_____

Meaning of the root word "fame":

_____

_____

_____

Meaning of the word "infamy":

_____

_____

_____

Meaning of the quote:

_____

_____

_____

**CHAPTER 6**

Illustrate the definitions of each Key Term. Then give one example of each term.

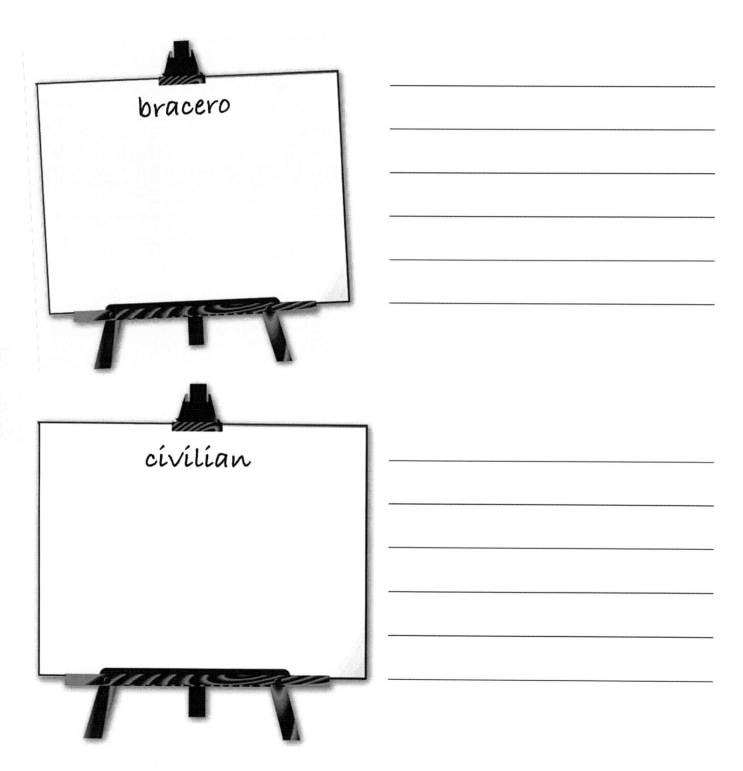

**New Mexicans Help Win World War II**    Lesson **2**    # Comprehension Strategy

## Infer and Question

As you read, record interesting facts from the lesson. After reading, revisit the facts and combine them with your visualizations to make inference statements about the lesson.

```
┌─────────────────────────────────────────────────────────┐
│                      Lesson Title                         │
│                                                           │
│                                                           │
│                                                           │
│                                                           │
└─────────────────────────────────────────────────────────┘
```

```
┌─────────────────────────────────────────────────────────┐
│             What you already know about the topic:        │
│                                                           │
│                                                           │
│                                                           │
│                                                           │
└─────────────────────────────────────────────────────────┘
```

CHAPTER 6

```
┌──────────────────────────┐  ┌──────────────────────────┐
│         Questions         │  │        Inferences         │
│                           │  │                           │
│                           │  │                           │
│                           │  │                           │
│                           │  │                           │
│                           │  │                           │
│                           │  │                           │
│                           │  │                           │
│                           │  │                           │
└──────────────────────────┘  └──────────────────────────┘
```

New Mexicans Help
Win World War II

Lesson 2

**Application** (page 1 of 2)

## WWII Learning Wheel

To show what you have learned from this lesson, make a learning wheel. Trace or cut out the circles on both activity pages. For each section of the first circle, write three facts about the Key Idea. Once the circles are complete, place a brad through the center of the two circles.

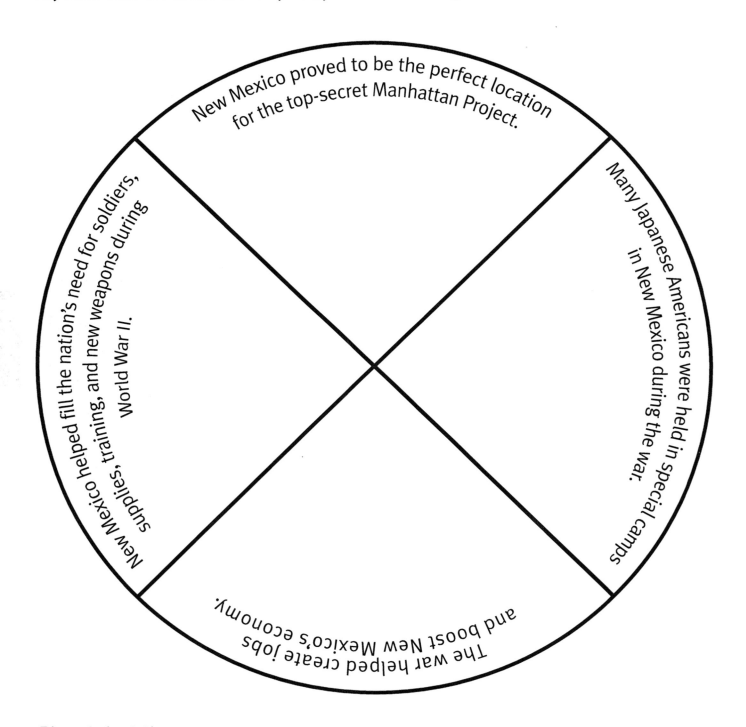

New Mexico proved to be the perfect location for the top-secret Manhattan Project.

New Mexico helped fill the nation's need for soldiers, supplies, training, and new weapons during World War II.

Many Japanese Americans were held in special camps in New Mexico during the war.

The war helped create jobs and boost New Mexico's economy.

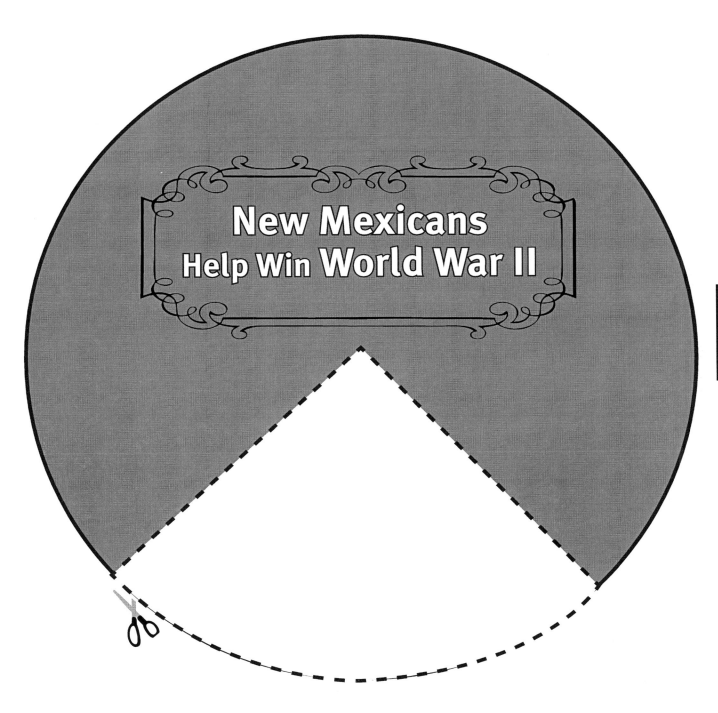

New Mexicans
Help Win World War II

CHAPTER 6

## The Cold War

What do you think the Cold War was? Complete the acrostic poem by writing one word for each letter in *THE COLD WAR* to describe what you think the Cold War was.

**T** _____

**H** _____

**E** _____

**C** _____

**O** _____

**L** _____

**D** _____

**W** _____

**A** _____

**R** _____

**New Mexico and the Cold War**    Lesson **3**

# Key Terms

Complete the table with information about the Key Terms from the lesson. In the Words to Describe column, list adjectives, key words, or phrases that will help you remember the Key Terms. Then give examples of each Key Term in the Examples column.

| Key Terms | Words to Describe | Examples |
|---|---|---|
| arms race | | |
| capitalism | | |
| cold war | | |
| communism | | |
| propaganda | | |
| superpower | | |

CHAPTER 6

New Mexico
and the Cold War     Lesson      # Comprehension Strategy

## Infer Meaning of New Words

Before reading the lesson, read around each of the Key Terms to gather details about their meanings. Use the details to infer the meaning of each term. While reading, list at least two words that are new to you. Read around the words to gather details and make inferences about their meanings. After reading, compare your inferences to the actual meaning of the words.

| Key Term or New Word | Details From the Lesson | Inferred Meaning |
|---|---|---|
| | | |

**New Mexico and the Cold War**    Lesson **3**    **Application**

## Dear Journal

Write a journal entry as if you were alive when the Cold War ended. Use information from the lesson to explain what caused the Cold War, the events during the war, and how the war ended.

*Dear Journal,*

_____

_____

_____

_____

_____

_____

_____

_____

_____

_____

_____

_____

_____

_____

_____

**CHAPTER 6**

## All Men Are Created Equal

**Read part of Dr. Martin Luther King's speech below, and list some of the rights you have as teenagers today.**

I say to you today, my friends, that in spite of the difficulties and frustrations of the moment, I still have a dream. It is a dream deeply rooted in the American dream.

I have a dream that one day this nation will rise up and live out the true meaning of its creed: "We hold these truths to be self-evident: that all men are created equal."

I have a dream that one day on the red hills of Georgia the sons of former slaves and the sons of former slaveowners will be able to sit down together at a table of brotherhood.

I have a dream that one day even the state of Mississippi, a desert state, sweltering with the heat of injustice and oppression, will be transformed into an oasis of freedom and justice.

I have a dream that my four children will one day live in a nation where they will not be judged by the color of their skin but by the content of their character.

I have a dream today.

Rights I Have:

_____          _____

_____          _____

_____          _____

_____          _____

_____          _____

**Challenge and Change** Lesson  **Key Terms**

Follow the directions to create a word-report poster for the Key Terms from this lesson.

**Include each of the Key Terms on your poster:**

- activist
- boycott
- discrimination
- diversity
- integration
- labor union
- minority
- segregation

**Choose three items to include on your poster for each of the Key Terms:**

1. Define each term.
2. Draw a picture to represent each term.
3. Describe the term in your own words.
4. Use the term in a sentence.
5. Give an example of each term from the lesson.
6. Give an example of each term from your own life.
7. Give a meaning that is opposite of the meaning of each term.
8. Explain how you think each term could be used today.

CHAPTER 6

## Infer to Finish the Story

As you read about each event in the lesson, infer as to how you think the event will end. Read to learn how the event really ends. Compare your inferences to the details from the lesson. Were your inferences accurate?

| Event | How I Think It Ends | How It Really Ends |
|---|---|---|
|  |  |  |

**Challenge and Change**     Lesson                     ## Application

## Fighting for Rights

Blacks, Hispanics, and Native Americans all struggled for civil rights. Use information from this lesson to describe how each group was discriminated against and what they each did to fight for their rights. Be detailed and give specific answers.

| Blacks |
|---|
|  |

| Hispanics |
|---|
|  |

| Native Americans |
|---|
|  |

**Why Is Government Necessary?**    Lesson **1**               **Activator**

## Why Government?

The pyramid represents each level of government we have in the United States. Use the pyramid to answer the questions.

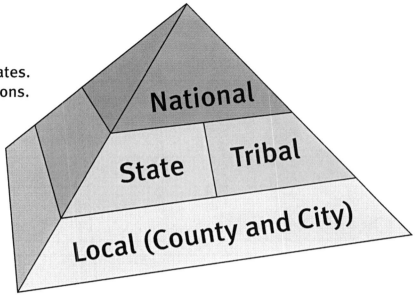

1. Why do we have four different types of government?

_____

_____

2. Why is the bottom level, local government, larger than the top level, national government?

_____

_____

3. Is one level of government more important than the others? Why or why not?

_____

_____

4. Why do we need each level of government?

_____

_____

**CHAPTER 7**

**Why Is Government Necessary?**   Lesson **1**                    **Key Terms**

Complete the table with information about the Key Terms from this chapter.

| KEY TERMS | WORDS TO DESCRIBE | EXAMPLES |
| --- | --- | --- |
| amendment | | |
| Bill of Rights | | |
| checks and balances | | |
| civics | | |
| democracy | | |
| federal system | | |
| municipality | | |
| ordinance | | |
| public goods | | |
| republic | | |

## Web of Main Ideas

After reading the lesson, choose a main heading in the lesson and create a web of main ideas for it. Revisit the lesson to help you find details.

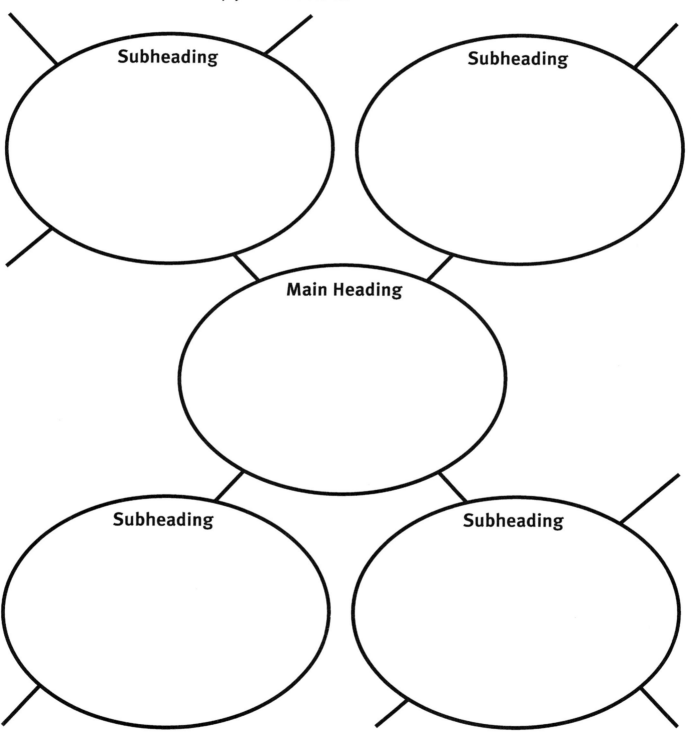

**CHAPTER 7**

**Why Is Government Necessary?**  Lesson **1**                    **Application**

## Why We Need Government
Use the pyramid and information from the lesson to answer the questions.

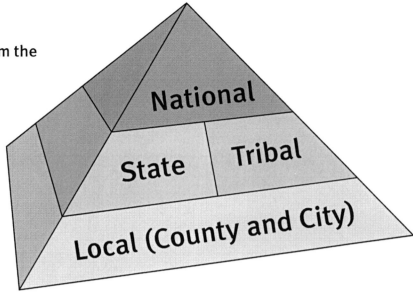

National

State     Tribal

Local (County and City)

**1.** Why do we have four different types of government?

_____

_____

**2.** Why is the bottom level, local government, larger than the top level, national government?

_____

_____

**3.** Is one level of government more important than the others? Why or why not?

_____

_____

**4.** Why do we need each level of government?

_____

_____

How Government Works   Lesson ❷                                    **Activator**

## Different Levels and Branches

Use the word bank to complete the table with the missing information for each level and branch of government. In the first column, name the title of office. In the second column, identify the parts of the Legislative Branch. In the third column, identify the type of court.

| National, State, and Local Government Organizations | | | |
|---|---|---|---|
| | **Executive** | **Legislative** | **Judicial** |
| **National** | President | | U.S. Supreme Court |
| **State** | | State Senate and State House of Representatives | |
| **County** | | | |
| **City or Town** | | City Council | |
| **Tribal** | Chairperson | | Tribal Courts |

### Word Bank

Governor

County Executive

Mayor and/or City Manager

U.S. Senate and U.S. House of Representatives

County Commissioners

Tribal Council

Washington Supreme Court, Supreme Court of Appeals

Superior Court, Juvenile Court, District Court

Municipal Courts

CHAPTER 7

Use the clues below to unscramble each Key Term.

**cealrl**

A _____ is a form of direct democracy that allows citizens to remove elected officials from office.

**lrcmbaeia**

A _____ government has two legislative chambers, or houses.

**tericd oemycadrc**

A _____ _____ is a type of government where citizens are directly involved in the lawmaking process rather than electing representatives.

**toev**

_____ is the power of a president or governor to reject a bill proposed by a legislature.

**ilbl**

A written proposal for a law is called a _____.

**dmrrenefue**

A _____ is a form of direct democracy that allows citizens to vote on laws passed or constitutional amendments approved by the legislature.

**naeiiittiv**

A form of direct democracy where citizens draft a law or constitutional amendment that will be put on the ballot for the action of the voters is called an _____.

**Pictures can help you remember what words mean. Choose three of the more difficult Key Terms to illustrate on another sheet of paper.**

## Make an Outline of Main Ideas

Use information from the lesson to complete the outline. Parts of the outline are done for you to help make sure you are doing it correctly.

**Lesson Title: How Government Works**

**I.** The Executive Branch

A. _____

B. _____

C. _____

**II.** _____

A. _____

B. _____

C. _____

D. Legislative Responsibilities _____

E. _____

**III.** _____

A. _____

**IV.** _____

A. _____

B. _____

**CHAPTER 7**

How Government Works    Lesson **2**    **Comprehension Strategy** (page 2 of 2)

**V.** The Judicial Branch

A. _____

B. _____

C. _____

D. _____

**VI.**

A. _____

_____

B. _____

_____

C. _____

_____

D. _____

_____

E. _____

_____

F. _____

_____

How Government Works    Lesson  2                    **Application**

## Why Not Just One?

Complete the table and use information from the lesson to describe the responsibilities of each branch and level of government in your own words. Briefly explain why we have different branches and levels of government instead of just one branch and one level. Include whether or not you think this is the best way to govern a democracy and why.

| National, State, and Local Government Organizations | | | |
|---|---|---|---|
| | Executive | Legislative | Judicial |
| National | President | | U.S. Supreme Court |
| State | | State Senate and State House of Representatives | |
| County | | | |
| City or Town | | City Council | |
| Tribal | Chairperson | | Tribal Courts |

_____

_____

_____

_____

_____

_____

CHAPTER 7

**Understanding Economics**     Lesson **1**

# Activator

## Do You Know Economics?

Fill out the chart by writing what you know about each topic.

| Trading | |
|---|---|
| **Money and Spending Options** | |
| **Interest** | |
| **Banks** | |

CHAPTER 8

**Understanding Economics**     Lesson  **1**                                    **Key Terms**

Using the Key Terms from the Word Bank, unscramble
the terms below. Then create a short story using each
of the Key Terms.

> **Word Bank**
>
> barter        deposit
> coerce        economics
> consumer      interest
> currency      producer

1. runycerc _____

2. rsteteni _____

3. nmcsiooec _____

4. rretab _____

5. uermnsoc _____

6. oitsepd _____

7. eecroc _____

8. rdcreuop _____

_____

_____

_____

_____

_____

_____

_____

_____

_____

Understanding Economics — Lesson  1

# Comprehension Strategy

## Two-Column Notes

As you read the lesson, take notes in the left column. After reading, revisit your notes to record more details in the right column. Be sure your notes are in your own words.

| Notes | Revisit Notes |
|---|---|
|  |  |

CHAPTER 8

Use with *The New Mexico Journey*

**Application**

## New Mexico's Economy and You

Now is your chance to share how you are a part of New Mexico's economy! In the first chart, list the products you consume as well as the forms of spending that were used to purchase the products. In the second chart, list the products you produce. Be prepared to answer questions about your charts.

| I am a CONSUMER of . . . | |
| --- | --- |
| PRODUCTS | FORM OF SPENDING USED |
|  |  |

| I am a PRODUCER of... |
| --- |
| PRODUCTS |
|  |

**Free Enterprise**     Lesson **2**                                    **Activator**

## Goods and Services

Write "G" for jobs that have to do with the creation of a good and "S" for jobs that provide a service. After reading the lesson, revisit this page to make any changes.

| | | | |
|---|---|---|---|
| | 1. Fixing the plumbing | | 2. Teaching students |
| | 3. Making engines for cars | | 4. Delivering newspapers |
| | 5. Checking people into hotel rooms | | 6. Cutting hair |
| | 7. Painting houses | | 8. Mowing lawns |
| | 9. Making cars | | 10. Making greeting cards |

Now it is your turn! Think about goods and services that you and your family use. Perhaps you pay someone to mow your lawn. That is a service. Maybe you stopped by a farm to buy some apples. Apples are a good. List goods and services used by you and your family.

| GOODS | SERVICES |
|---|---|
| | |
| | |
| | |
| | |
| | |
| | |

**CHAPTER 8**

Use with *The New Mexico Journey*

**Free Enterprise**          Lesson **2**                    **Key Terms**

Fill out the chart by writing two or three key words from the definition that will help you remember the Key Terms. Then draw a quick sketch to help you remember each definition.

| KEY TERM | KEY WORDS | SKETCH |
|---|---|---|
| demand | | |
| free enterprise | | |
| profit | | |
| shortage | | |
| supply | | |
| surplus | | |

**Free Enterprise**          Lesson           # Comprehension Strategy

## The Cornell Method

Use the organizer to take notes as you study the lesson. Be sure your notes are in your own words. Remember, they do not need to be complete sentences.

| 2. Reduce or Question (After Reading)<br>• From your notes at the right, list key words, phrases or questions that serve as cues for notes taken in class<br><br>(Cue phrases and questions should be in your own words) | 1. Record (During Reading)<br>• Using your own words and phrasing, list facts, details, and ideas you pick up from the reading<br><br>(Use abbreviations when possible) |
|---|---|
| 3. Recite<br>• Cover your notes on the right and read each key word or question<br><br>• Recite the fact or idea brought to mind by key word or question | |
| | (After Reading)<br>• Read through your notes, make corrections, and identify abbreviations<br><br><br>4. & 5. Reflect and Review<br>• Review your notes periodically by repeating step 3<br>• Add additional notes if necessary |

**6. Recap**
• Summarize each main idea (Use complete sentences)

CHAPTER 8

© 2012 Gibbs Smith Education
Use with *The New Mexico Journey*

**Free Enterprise**   Lesson  2          **Application**

## Three Scenarios of Business

You are the owner of an athletic shoe store. Read each scenario and use information from the lesson to decide how much you will charge in each situation. Be sure to include the reason why you will charge each price.

### SCENARIO 1

Athletic shoes have been made in many stores in your city and only one store is selling them at a very cheap price.

_____

_____

_____

_____

### SCENARIO 2

You are the only store in your city that is selling athletic shoes but not many people are buying them.

_____

_____

_____

_____

### SCENARIO 3

You are one of two stores who sell athletic shoes, and these shoes are in very high demand by consumers in your community.

_____

_____

_____

_____

**Working in New Mexico**    Lesson **3**                  **Activator**

## Businesses in New Mexico

Many different businesses work together to make New Mexico a great place to live! Choose one local business to learn more about. Fill out the activity page. Use it to help you write the business a letter.

| The local business I want to learn more about is: _____ |
| --- |

**1.** What do I already know about this business's goods or services?

_____

_____

**2.** What do I want to know about this business's goods or services?

_____

_____

_____

**3.** What do I already know about this business's renewable and non-renewable resources?

_____

_____

**4.** What do I want to know about this business's renewable and non-renewable resources?

_____

_____

_____

On a separate sheet of paper, write the business a letter. Tell them what you already know about them. Ask them questions about their business. Report your findings to the class.

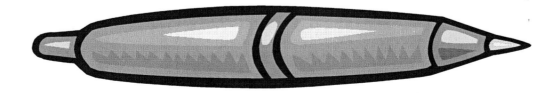

CHAPTER 8

**Working in New Mexico**     Lesson **3**                                 **Key Terms**

Fill in the blank with the **Key Term** that matches the definition.

aquifer          renewable          urbanization
interdependence  specialization
non-renewable    sustainability

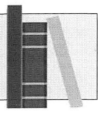

1. _____ a situation where people and businesses depend on one another to provide the things they do not produce themselves

2. _____ refers to activities that have little long-term impact on the environment

3. _____ the development of special skills and strengths in certain areas

4. _____ a deep, water-filled cavern

5. _____ resources that are unlimited or can be easily replenished

6. _____ the growth of cities

7. _____ resources that exist in a limited supply; not replaceable

**Use each of the Key Terms in a sentence.**

aquifer

_____

interdependence

_____

non-renewable

_____

renewable

_____

specialization

_____

sustainability

_____

urbanization

_____

## Determine the Importance

Use the organizer to help you determine which details of the lesson are the most important. Use details from the lesson to support your key concepts.

| Key Concepts (with page #s) | Concept in Your Own Words | Why the Concept is Important |
| --- | --- | --- |
|  |  |  |

## My Favorite Things

Brainstorm a list of your favorite products. Choose one of the products to research. Fill out the following information about your product and include a picture.

**MY FAVORITE THINGS**

_____     _____

_____     _____

_____     _____

_____     _____

**Product to Research:** _____

1. How my product was made: _____

_____

_____

_____

2. Materials used to make my product: _____

_____

_____

3. Where my product was made: _____

4. When my product was made: _____

Draw or glue a picture of your product below.